The Years I Lost ar
I'm Reclaiming

Dedication

To my four boys —
Samuel, Joshua, Joseph, and Oliver.
I gave you life,
but you gave me reason to live.

And to anyone who's ever been told they wouldn't make it —
This book is proof that you can.

Contents

1. The First Time I Chose Life

There's a part of my story most people still don't know — I nearly died from endocarditis.

I'd just been remanded into custody at Styal Prison. I knew something wasn't right. I'd felt ill for weeks, but like always, I pushed through it. I thought it was just withdrawal. Maybe stress. Maybe both. And then everything went black.

I don't remember being blue-lighted to hospital. I don't remember collapsing. I don't remember the first seven days of intensive care. That entire week is gone — a blank space in my life I'll never get back.

Nurses filled in the details later. Machines had been keeping me alive. They told me I was lucky to survive. They said if I'd arrived any later, I wouldn't be here. That I was a breath away from open heart surgery. That the infection — infective endocarditis — had nearly taken me out.

And still, I couldn't quite grasp it. I was dazed. Weak. But alive.

When they told me straight — "You need to stop using. Or you're going to die." — there was no room left to argue.

I didn't feel brave. I felt broken. But I knew that if I carried on, I'd just be another name on a tag. Another forgotten girl who never got the chance to become more.

That hospital bed was where I made my first real choice in years. Not for heroin. Not for chaos. But for life.

It wasn't clean or pretty. Detox nearly killed me too. But I did it.

I chose life.

And that's when everything began to change.

2. When I Spoke Up

I was sixteen the first time I spoke the truth out loud.

I didn't plan it. It wasn't some big, brave moment. It spilled out of me in pieces — broken words, jagged edges, fear wrapped in silence. I told someone what my dad had been doing to me. The thing I'd buried. The thing I thought I'd take to the grave.

And to my shock, I was believed.

That should've felt like relief. It didn't.

It felt like everything was crumbling.

Because when you speak the truth about something so dark, something that's been hidden for so long, you don't just free yourself — you break everything around you. The silence that held it all together shatters, and suddenly everyone's looking. Judging. Reacting.

I wasn't met with comfort or protection. Not from the people who should have loved me. My 'mum' didn't hold me. She didn't fight for me. She turned away. I wasn't her daughter in that moment. I was an inconvenience. A threat to the version of life she wanted to keep pretending was normal.

I didn't feel strong. I felt like a problem. Like I'd ruined everything.

And the weight of it all was too much. I spiraled. I wanted out.

That's how I ended up sectioned under the Mental Health Act. A Section 3. Locked away at sixteen years old because I'd tried to end my life.

Not because I was broken. But because I felt like no one cared that I was finally telling the truth.

I wasn't put in hospital because I lied.

I was put there because I told the truth and couldn't cope with what came next.

My dad went to prison for what he did. People say that means justice was served. Maybe on paper. But what about the pieces of me that never got put back together? What about the girl left behind, locked in a hospital ward, convinced she was the one who'd done something wrong?

I survived what he did to me.

Then I survived what came after.

And that's why this chapter matters.

Because there's power in speaking up — even when it almost breaks you.

3. The Girl on Section 3

I was just a girl when they sectioned me — sixteen years old but already carrying a lifetime of damage.

Section 3 of the Mental Health Act. That's not just a phrase. It's a sentence. A locked door. A label. I wasn't being treated; I was being contained. For my own good, they said. But it didn't feel like help. It felt like punishment for surviving.

The ward was cold, clinical. Everything was white and grey, like even the walls had been drained of feeling. I wasn't allowed to leave. I wasn't allowed to cry without being watched. I wasn't allowed to scream without it becoming a "behavioral incident." I wasn't even allowed to feel like a child — because once you're on Section 3, you're no longer a girl. You're a risk. A problem. A diagnosis.

I didn't go in there because I was unstable. I went in there because I told the truth about what my dad did to me, and the world didn't know what to do with it. I was falling apart, and instead of being held, I was locked up.

There were other girls there too. All of us broken in our own way. We bonded through shared glances, whispered conversations, passing each other pens when the staff weren't looking. We weren't friends, not really. Just co-survivors in a place built to keep us from feeling anything too loudly.

I spent weeks in that hospital. Sometimes I wonder how I got out — not physically, but mentally. I was so deep in that darkness. So sure that I wasn't worth saving.

But somewhere inside me, even then, was this tiny flicker of something stubborn. A voice that whispered, "You're not done yet."

And that's what kept me breathing.

The girl on Section 3 didn't think she had a future. She didn't see hope. But she survived. And I wish I could say that was the turning point. That I left hospital and everything got better.

But that's not how it went.

I left one kind of prison and walked straight into another. I found heroin. Or maybe it found me. Either way, it wrapped itself around me like a false comfort, promising peace and delivering chaos. I was still searching for silence, still trying to numb what I couldn't cope with. And heroin was the easiest way to forget.

So, no — I didn't make it out clean. But I made it out alive.

And that's something.

4. The Mother I Didn't Have

When people talk about mothers, they talk about love. Not the big, flashy kind — the quiet, consistent kind. The kind that makes you feel safe without needing to be said out loud. And yes, my mum did some of those things. She made sure I had clean clothes. There was always tea on the table. She packed my school bag, sent me off with lunch. From the outside, we looked fine.

But it was what I didn't get that shaped me the most.

I grew up with someone who gave me life but didn't know how to nurture it. She wasn't physically abusive. She made sure I had the basics. But emotionally? I was on my own. There were no warm hugs. No gentle encouragement. No space to talk about feelings. And when I tried, it was met with coldness — or worse, silence.

I never felt like her daughter. I felt like her burden. Sometimes, I even felt like her rival — like there wasn't enough space in the house for two women, and I'd somehow been cast in the role of 'other woman' rather than child.

When I told the truth about what my dad had done, she didn't stand beside me. She didn't wrap me in love or shield me from the fallout. She disappeared emotionally, turned cold, distant — like I'd shattered the image she was trying to protect. And maybe I had. But that wasn't on me.

Sometimes I think she didn't choose him. I think she chose herself. Survival. Image. Denial. Whatever it was, it wasn't me.

We've got something now. A version of a relationship. We speak. We manage. But we're not close. And I've learned not to expect warmth where there's never been any. It's still hard, though. Because I grieve for what I never had — a mother I could run to, cry to, lean on.

If she ever reads this, she'll focus on how I made her look. Not how I felt. That's always been the way.

But this chapter isn't about blame. It's about truth. My truth.

Because I know how it feels to grow up craving softness and getting silence.

And that's why I'm different with my boys. I show up. I listen. I love out loud. I hold them when they cry and celebrate when they thrive. I tell them I'm proud — because I am.

I became the mother I didn't have.

And that's something I'll always be proud of.

5. The Streets Don't Let You Forget

The streets have a memory — and they never let you forget.

Once you've been out there, really out there, it stays with you. It gets in your bones. It follows you even when you think you've moved on. You can walk a straight path for years, but the streets still whisper your name when life gets hard.

When I hit the streets, I wasn't running toward freedom. I was running from pain. From a home that didn't feel safe. From a past that wouldn't leave me alone. I thought I was choosing independence. What I found was chaos.

I learned to survive in places that most people pretend don't exist. Couch-surfing turned into sleeping rough. Drugs blurred the edges. The days bled into nights. Some people don't understand what it takes to survive the decisions you make, the things you see, the parts of yourself you trade just to stay warm or get through another night.

You stop looking in mirrors. You stop caring about birthdays. Everything becomes about getting through the next hour.

But there's a weird kind of community out there too. I met people who'd give you their last tenner, even if they were shaking for a fix themselves. People with stories just as sad, just as messy. We became a family of misfits. No rules. No judgement. Just survival.

But the thing about that life is... it never let's go easy.

Even now, I'll Walk through town and clock a familiar face — someone I used to run with. Some of them are gone. Some are stuck. Some look straight through me like they can't believe I got out.

And that guilt creeps in. Because not everyone makes it.

Because part of me still remembers what it felt like to be that girl with nothing.

I don't glamorize it. There was nothing beautiful about waking up cold, hungry, and broken. But it happened. And it's part of me.

The streets taught me how to survive.

But they also nearly killed me.

6. The Years I Lost and the Life I'm Reclaiming

I lost years. That's not just a phrase — it's a reality. Whole chunks of my life blurred by addiction, trauma, self-destruction. There are birthdays I missed. People I hurt. Days I can't get back. And for a long time, I believed I didn't deserve to.

There's a kind of grief that comes with recovery. Not just for what happened — but for all the things that never did. The girl I never got to be. The milestones I never reached. The version of me that might have existed if life had been different.

But grief isn't the end of the story.

Because I didn't stay lost.

I clawed my way back from places most people don't return from. I fought to stay alive, even when I didn't care if I did. I chose recovery when I could have chosen to disappear. And that decision — that fight — became the start of everything.

It wasn't clean. It wasn't straight. I slipped. I relapsed. I hurt people. I hurt myself. There were days I didn't care if I made it through. Times when survival felt like punishment. But somewhere inside me, something kept whispering, "You're not done yet."

It wasn't about suddenly being good or strong. It was about refusing to give up — even when I had every reason to. And slowly, piece by piece, I started building something that looked like a life. One I could live with. One I could be proud of.

I started remembering who I was before the world broke me — and imagining who I could be after. I stopped trying to disappear and started trying to heal. I learned how to carry my past without letting it define me. I learned how to speak without shame. I learned how to stand up — even on shaking legs.

The years I lost? I'll never get them back.

But the life I'm building now? That's mine.

And I'm not giving it up for anything.

7. The Love That Hurt and the Peace That Followed

When I got clean, I was at my most fragile.

My body was healing, but my spirit was still shattered.

I was raw. Trying to rebuild a life with no blueprint.

So when he came into my world, I thought maybe I'd found someone who could help me feel whole again.

He met me at rock bottom.

Fresh out of addiction.

Unsure of who I was without the chaos, unsure if I even deserved calm.

I was easy to shape — because I didn't know my worth yet.

At first, it felt like safety.

Like someone had finally chosen me.

But slowly, I began to shrink.

My confidence — the little I had — was chipped away.

I stopped laughing.

Stopped trusting myself.

Started believing that maybe this was as good as I'd get.

It wasn't obvious from the outside.

It wasn't something you'd spot in a photo.

But it was there — in the way I second-guessed myself, walked on eggshells, forgot how to be me.

It was rough.

Emotionally draining.

Lonely, even when I wasn't alone.

And yet... I stayed.

Because I thought this was the price of love.

Because I had children to think of.

Because when you've spent years feeling like nothing, you stop asking for more.

Eventually, I found my strength.

I left.

Not because it was easy — but because I had to.

Because I wanted my boys to see what self-respect looked like.

And now, here's what surprises people:

We're friends.

Not close, not emotional — but civil. Focused. Mature.

Because we're parents first.

We co-parent for the sake of our children.

And no matter what happened between us, the kids matter more than ego or history.

It might look strange from the outside — but for us, it works.

It's not about pretending nothing happened.

It's about choosing peace over conflict.

Choosing the bigger picture.

And even though those years stripped me down, they didn't break me.

They reminded me what I wouldn't accept again.

They showed me what love should never cost.

Now I parent with clarity.

I hold my own.

And I teach my kids that relationships should never make you feel small.

That chapter is closed — not with bitterness, but with boundaries.

And that's enough.

8. The Moment I Left

Leaving Alan wasn't some brave, planned decision.

It wasn't a "lightbulb moment" or an act of sudden empowerment.

It was forced. It was urgent.

We had an argument — one of many.

But this one was different. It exploded.

Words flew, threats were made, and something in the air shifted.

The police got involved. Then social services.

And suddenly, I was no longer just a woman in a toxic relationship — I was a mum under scrutiny.

They didn't sugarcoat it.

"If you don't leave him, you could lose your kids."

That sentence hit harder than anything he'd ever said or done.

It wasn't that I didn't already know things were bad — I did.

But hearing it out loud, from someone with authority, made it real.

Undeniable. Unavoidable.

All the excuses I'd used to justify staying —

That he'd change.

That he was hurting too.

That I was the problem.

That it was better for the kids to have two parents.

They didn't matter anymore.

None of it did.

Because now, my children were watching.

And if I didn't act, I wasn't just letting myself down — I was failing them.

So, I left.

Not in defiance.

Not with pride.

Not even with strength, if I'm honest.

I left because I had no choice.

Because survival had to come before love.

Because my children deserved better.

Because deep down, some part of me knew I deserved better too — even if I didn't fully believe it yet.

And what surprised me most?

He didn't fight for me.

He didn't beg me to stay.

No grand gesture. No apology. Just silence.

And that silence said everything.

It confirmed what I'd been too scared to admit — that he never really loved me. Not in the way I needed to be loved. Not in the way that healed or lifted or protected.

I walked out of that chapter of my life with nothing but my name and my kids.

And for the first time in years, that was enough.

I left because I had to.

But I stayed gone because, finally, I realised

I was worth saving too.

9. The Noise That Comes Back

You don't just walk away from trauma. You carry it — in your skin, in your bones, in your nervous system. In the way your body tenses when someone raises their voice. In the way you flinch at kindness because you're not sure it's real.

I have Complex Post-Traumatic Stress Disorder — C-PTSD — and it's not just a label. It's a lens through which I experience the world. My past isn't just behind me. It lingers in the present, always there, always buzzing beneath the surface.

I left the relationship. I got clean. I rebuilt my life. But the noise — the flashbacks, the panic, the guilt — that didn't disappear. Sometimes it's triggered by nothing at all. Sometimes it's a smell, a word, a change in someone's tone. Suddenly, I'm not a grown woman — I'm a scared girl again, stuck in memories I can't control.

I've smiled through panic attacks. Held conversations while my chest was tight and my hands were shaking. I've made packed lunches, done school runs, and read bedtime stories while silently battling a war in my own head.

People think trauma looks loud — like screaming or sobbing. But sometimes it's quiet. It's withdrawal. Numbness. Detachment. And surviving it takes energy most people don't even realise you're spending.

There've been times I've ended up in hospital, not from physical wounds, but because the noise got too loud to carry alone. I'd shut down. Become unreachable. And every time it happened, a part of me would feel ashamed — like I was failing, even after everything I'd already overcome.

But trauma doesn't care how far you've come. C-PTSD doesn't just disappear because life looks more stable now. It waits. Quietly. And it shows up when you're tired, vulnerable, or when things go still for too long.

I don't think I'll ever be fully "free" of it. This is part of me now. But it's not all of me.

I've learned to name it. To face it. To manage it.

Some days I still stare at the ceiling and wonder if I'll ever feel light again. But even in those moments, I know one thing for sure — I'm not broken.

I'm surviving. I'm healing. I'm showing up.

And that counts.

10. The Mother I Chose to Become

I didn't grow up with the kind of mum I needed.

Affection didn't come easily. Warmth wasn't a given.

There were no late-night heart-to-hearts, no arms that felt like safety.

I wasn't protected the way a daughter should be.

So when I became a mother myself, I felt two things:

Love so big it scared me — and fear I'd never be enough.

Because how do you mother when no one mothered you?

But here's what I learned —

You get to choose what kind of mum you become.

And I chose to be different.

I chose to be the mum who listens.

Who says sorry when she gets it wrong.

Who shows up — not perfectly, but honestly.

Who says "I love you" out loud and often.

I've had to learn as I go.

There's no manual for parenting through trauma.

There've been days where I've cried after school runs, nights where I doubted every decision.

Sometimes I shout. Sometimes I freeze. Sometimes I overthink bedtime routines because I want everything to feel safe for them.

But still — I try.

I fight my demons so they won't have to fight the same ones.

I go to therapy. I check myself. I apologise when I mess up. Because I know what it's like to grow up feeling like a burden, and I refuse to let my boys carry that feeling.

Motherhood hasn't healed me, but it's given me purpose.

They're my reason — not my crutch, not my identity — but my anchor.

They don't need a perfect mum.

They need a real one.

And that, I can be.

11. The Art That Saved Me

I'm not sure I would've survived without creativity.

I didn't always realise it at the time, but making things — anything — helped me cope.

It started with scrapbooks. Nothing fancy. Just pages filled with quotes, photos, memories — things that helped me make sense of the chaos. I liked having control over something. Picking what stayed. What didn't. It felt like therapy in its own way.

Then there were my tattoos.

They're not just ink. They're my story, written on skin I used to hate.

My big Mother Goose tattoo, with four little goslings behind her — that's for my boys. It means everything to me. It says, "I've got you. I'll protect you. Always."

The flowers are for them too — a symbol that something beautiful can grow out of the darkest soil.

Then there's the owl — wise, silent, always watching. That one sits proudly on my back.

And on my wrist is a bold budgie — not tiny at all, and not subtle either. That's for my grandma. She loved budgies. She was soft, patient, the kind of gentle I didn't get much of growing up. That tattoo reminds me she's still with me. Close. Holding on, even now.

There was also a time I got into photography. I liked seeing the world through a different lens — literally. It helped me slow down and notice things. Light. Shadows. Smiles. It gave me perspective. Some of my favourite memories are tied to the photos I took when life finally started to feel lighter.

People ask what all these things mean — the art, the tattoos, the pictures.

The truth is, they helped me stay alive.

They helped me feel when I'd gone numb.

They helped me remember who I am, even when I forgot.

I don't create to impress anyone.

I do it to breathe. To process. To survive.

This is how I honour my past.

This is how I move forward.

Art didn't save me all at once. But it's saved me in little ways, over and over again.

12. The Teacher I'm Becoming

If you'd told me years ago that I'd end up in a classroom, I'd have laughed.

Not because I didn't want it — but because I never thought I deserved it.

I didn't see myself as someone who could lead, inspire, or teach.

I saw someone who'd been broken, thrown away, written off.

But life had other plans.

And slowly, step by step, I started showing up — not just for others, but for myself.

It started small.

Helping out at school. Reading with kids.

Then came volunteering. More responsibility. More belief in myself.

Until eventually, I realised... I'm good at this. I care. I connect. And I matter.

The classroom feels like a second home now.

I've spent years helping children believe in themselves while learning to do the same.

They've taught me just as much as I've taught them — patience, presence, resilience.

I don't take this journey for granted.

Because I know what it took to get here.

I carry my past with me — not as shame, but as a reminder.

It helps me spot the quiet ones, the anxious ones, the ones who act out because no one's ever shown them patience.

I see them. Because I was them.

And now, as I work towards becoming a qualified teacher, it's more than just ticking boxes or getting a degree.

It's about proving to myself — and maybe others too — that you can rewrite your story.

That you can come from hell and still build something good.

I'm not trying to be the perfect teacher.

I just want to be a safe one. A real one.

Someone who shows up, tells the truth, and helps kids believe in second chances — because I've lived one.

13. The Friendships I Struggle With But Still Crave

This has always been the hardest part for me — friendships.

I crave connection. I want people around me. I want to feel like I belong somewhere.

But I've never really known how to hold on to people, not properly.

I've had friends. I've been the friend who shows up, who listens, who tries.

But somewhere along the way, I always pull back. I get quiet. I overthink.

I convince myself I'm too much, or not enough.

Sometimes I ghost people before they can ghost me.

Sometimes I sit with my phone in my hand, staring at a message I'll never send.

Sometimes I get left out — and that just confirms the story I already tell myself.

It's not that I don't want connection. I do.

But trauma makes you guarded.

When you've spent years being let down, or hurt, or overlooked — trusting people becomes a risk you don't always know how to take.

Even now, working in school, I still struggle with it.

I've volunteered for three years. I've shown up, supported the kids, and done everything I can to be part of the team.

But most of the time, I still feel like "the parent." Not "one of them."

They're friendly. They include me in school life. But when it comes to the social stuff — the meals out, the parties, the little gatherings — I'm not on the list.

The first time I was ever invited to something was recently.

Three years in.

And as grateful as I was, it still hurt to realise how long I'd waited to be seen in that way.

It's not jealousy. It's longing.

And I know I'm not the only one.

Because friendship isn't always about big groups and girls' nights and endless laughter.

Sometimes it's just someone checking in. Someone remembering your birthday. Someone saving you a seat.

That's what I want.

I don't need a crowd. I need real.

And I'm still learning that I don't have to shrink myself to keep people.

That the right ones will understand the silences. The cancellations. The fear.

That I deserve connection — even if I'm still healing.

14. What I Remember

There are things I remember so clearly, it's like they just happened yesterday.

And then there are big parts of my life that feel like a blur — too painful, too heavy, too far gone.

I remember fear.

The kind that settles in your chest and never quite leaves.

I remember confusion — being a child and knowing something wasn't right, but not knowing how to explain it.

I remember his face.

The way he looked at me.

How I used to freeze up, trying to become invisible.

I remember feeling like the problem.

Even after I spoke up. Even when I was believed.

Because when the people who are meant to love and protect you are the same ones who hurt you — it messes with your entire understanding of love, safety, and self-worth.

I remember being sectioned at sixteen.

Not because I was mad. But because I told the truth.

Because I tried to survive something that should never have happened in the first place.

Because I tried to end the pain in the only way I could see at the time — by trying to end me.

I remember hospital lights.

The weight of silence.

The feeling that I might never make it out of that place — or if I did, I wouldn't come out the same.

I remember how people looked at me.

Like I was broken. Like I was dangerous.

But I wasn't either. I was a girl who had seen too much, felt too much, and been let down by too many.

I remember being in rooms where decisions were made about me, but I wasn't really seen.

And I also remember the little things that kept me going:

A smile from a nurse. A quiet cup of tea. A window with light coming through it.

There's a lot I've blocked out — maybe to protect myself.

But what I do remember has shaped who I am.

It lives in my body. In my reactions. In the way I love, trust, and guard myself.

And as painful as it is, I hold space for those memories now.

Because pretending they didn't happen never helped me heal.

But naming them — claiming them — that's how I take the power back.

15. This Is Not the End

People like me aren't supposed to make it.

We're the ones they write off. The ones who get whispered about. The ones whose names are followed by sighs and sad looks.

But I'm still here. Louder than I was meant to be.

And softer in ways that took me years to learn.

This book doesn't have a happy-ever-after. It's not neat or tidy.

It's messy, raw, still unfolding.

But it's real. And it's mine.

I've lived through hell.

I've clawed my way out of situations that would've destroyed the old me.

I've felt like a failure. A ghost. A mistake.

And yet, I've also felt love. Joy. Peace.

Sometimes for a second. Sometimes for a season.

But enough to know that it's possible.

I still have bad days.

The trauma doesn't just vanish.

The flashbacks, the shame, the doubt — they creep in when I least expect it.

But I've built better coping tools.

I ask for help now. I show up, even when it's hard. I keep choosing life.

I'm not here to inspire pity.

I'm here to reclaim every part of myself that I lost — and maybe help someone else believe they can do the same.

This isn't the end of my story.

It's just the part where I finally pick up the pen and write it my way.

Printed in Dunstable, United Kingdom